The Real Deal

EATING RIGHT

Barbara Sheen

Heinemann Library
Chicago, Illinois

Customer Service 888-454-2279
Visit our website at www.heinemannraintree.com

Designed by Richard Parker and Tinstar Design Ltd, www.tinstar.co.uk
Printed and bound in China by Leo Paper Group

12 11 10 09 08
10 9 8 7 6 5 4 3 2 1

Library of Congress Cataloging-in-Publication Data
Sheen, Barbara.
  Eating right / Barbara Sheen.
    p. cm. -- (The real deal)
  Includes bibliographical references and index.
  ISBN 978-1-4034-9694-2 (hardback : alk. paper) -- ISBN 978-1-4034-9701-7 (pbk. : alk. paper)
  1. Nutrition--Juvenile literature. I. Title.
  RA784.S5224 2008
  613.2--dc22
                          2007011174

Acknowledgments
The publishers would like to thank the following for permission to reproduce photographs: Action Images/John Marsh/Livepic p. 4; Alamy pp. 10 (don jon red), 12 (StockAB), 13 (Chuck Pefley), 23 (mediacolor's); Anthony Blake pp. 5, 16; Art Directors/Helene Rogers p. 21; Corbis pp. 20 (zefa/H. Schmid), 24 (Image Source); Getty/Stone/Christopher Bissell p. 15; Getty Images News/Chris Jackson p. 18; PhotoLibrary pp. 22 (Creatas), 27 (Radius Images); Science Photo Library/Mauro Fermariello p. 25; SuperStock pp. 7 (Mauritius), 9 (Francisco Cruz), 14, 17, 19 (age fotostock); US Department of Agriculture p. 11.

Cover photograph of an arrow road sign reproduced with permission of iStockphoto/Nicholas Belton; cover photographs of a strawberry and an orange slice reproduced with permission of Getty Images/ PhotoDisc.

Every effort has been made to contact copyright holders of any material reproduced in this book. Any omissions will be rectified in subsequent printings if notice is given to the publishers.

The publishers would like to thank Nicole A. Clark for her help in the preparation of this book.

Contents

Some words are shown in bold, **like this**. You can find out what they mean by looking in the glossary.

Valuable Nutrients

The human body is amazing and complex. Like a race car, it needs fuel to run. A race car's fuel is gasoline, while the human body's fuel is food. Food supplies the body with **nutrients,** the natural substances that keep the body working properly. Nutrients are organized into six groups: **proteins**, **fats**, **carbohydrates**, **vitamins**, **minerals**, and water.

Each nutrient has a different job. To stay healthy, each person needs to get enough of each nutrient every day. Not getting enough of a nutrient, or getting too much of some nutrients, can affect a person's health.

Foods that are loaded with nutrients are **nutrient-dense** foods. However, no single food contains every nutrient. The only way for people to get all the nutrients they need is by eating a variety of nutrient-dense foods every day.

Like any machine, the body needs fuel to power it.

NEWSFLASH

Fiber is the part of fruits, vegetables, **grains**, beans, seeds, and nuts that cannot be digested. Fiber is not a nutrient, but it helps keep us healthy. Fiber keeps food moving through the digestive system. Studies show that it also helps prevent heart disease and colon cancer.

Proteins

The human body is made up of proteins. Smaller units called **amino acids** are the building blocks of proteins. They replace and repair the millions of **cells** that make up the body.

Meat, fish, poultry, eggs, milk, and soybeans contain different proteins. Because they have all the amino acids, they are complete proteins. Dried beans, corn, wheat, nuts, seeds, and rice also contain protein, but not the amino acids essential for cell-building.

A balanced diet made up of a variety of nutrient-dense foods fuels the body.

Top Tip

Complete proteins tend to come from animal products, but **vegetarians** can still get all the protein they need. By combining plant proteins, a complete protein can be made. For example, peanut butter on whole wheat bread, or bean soup and cornbread, can combine to make complete proteins.

Type of Fat	Main Source
Monounsaturated	Olive, canola, and peanut oils; olives; avocados; cashews, almonds, peanuts, and most other nuts
Polyunsaturated	Fish, nuts, grains
Saturated	Whole milk, butter, cheese, and ice cream; chocolate; red meat; coconuts, coconut milk, and coconut oil
Trans fatty acids	Most margarines; vegetable shortening; partially hydrogenated vegetable oil; many fast foods; most commercial baked goods

Monounsaturated and polyunsaturated fats help rid the body of cholesterol.

Fats

The body gets energy from fats. Fats also insulate the body and help keep it warm. In addition, fats carry some vitamins through the bloodstream. The body needs some fats, but too many fats can be unhealthy.

There are three kinds of fats: saturated, unsaturated, and **trans fatty acids** (often called "trans fats"). Trans fats and **saturated fats** are solid at room temperature. They contain a waxy substance called cholesterol. High levels of cholesterol can clog **blood vessels** and cause heart disease.

Meat and milk products contain saturated fats. Trans fats are found in **processed foods** such as chips, pastries, and margarine. Eating too many trans fats and saturated fats can cause health problems such as heart disease, stroke, cancer, **diabetes**, high blood pressure, and obesity. Obesity is a disorder in which people have more body fat than is healthy.

Unsaturated fats are liquid at room temperature. There are two types. Monounsaturated fats are found in certain oils, such as olive oil, canola oil, and peanut oil. Polyunsaturated fats are found in nuts, grains, and fish. Unsaturated fats help remove cholesterol from the body.

Carbohydrates

Energy also comes from carbohydrates. They come in two varieties—simple and complex. Many foods that contain complex carbohydrates are nutrient-dense. The body breaks them down slowly, so they give the body long-lasting energy. Potatoes, dried beans, nuts, and **whole grains** are rich in complex carbohydrates.

Sugary foods contain simple carbohydrates and few other nutrients. Eating too many simple carbohydrates can cause problems. Bacteria in the mouth changes sugar to an acid that causes cavities. Eating large amounts of **non-nutrient dense** foods is also linked to cancer and obesity.

Whole grains contain fiber and complex carbohydrates.

Top Tip

Sugar-rich foods such as candy and soft drinks contain simple carbohydrates. The body breaks simple carbohydrates down quickly. They give the body a short burst of energy. For energy that lasts, eat complex carbohydrates, which break down more slowly.

Vitamins

The body needs only small amounts of vitamins, but without them it would not work properly. Fruits, vegetables, milk, whole grains, nuts, beans, meats, and seafood are full of the vitamins the body needs.

The main vitamins are A, C, D, E, and K. The vitamin B family is also important. It includes vitamins B_6, B_{12}, thiamine, riboflavin, niacin, folic acid, and pantothenic acid. Vitamin A helps people see, especially at night. It may help fight infection, along with vitamins C, E, and the B vitamins. The B vitamins help the body get energy from food. Vitamin K helps the blood to clot.

Some vitamins, such as D, E, and K, can be stored in the body. Vitamins C and B cannot be stored in the body. They must be replaced every day.

Vitamins and minerals have many important jobs.

Vitamin or Mineral	What it does	Where to find it
Calcium	Helps build strong teeth and bones; helps blood clot	Dairy products, sardines, broccoli, and other dark green vegetables
Iron	Helps blood production	Liver, red meat, whole grains, shellfish, dark green vegetables
Potassium	Helps the nerves and heart	Oranges, bananas, meat, fish, potatoes, beans, cereal
Vitamin A	Helps keep eyes, skin, and hair healthy	Milk, butter, cheese, eggs, liver
Vitamin B_6	Important for the nervous system and blood production	Meat, vegetables, nuts, beans, fish, rice, yeast
Vitamin C	Helps build strong gums, teeth, and bones	Oranges and other citrus fruits, berries, peppers, cabbage
Vitamin D	Helps build strong teeth and bones	Milk, eggs, salmon, tuna, cod liver oil
Vitamin E	Helps blood production	Vegetable oil, grains
Zinc	Helps wounds heal	Meat, whole grains, milk, beans

Vitamins and minerals help maintain a strong body and help people get energy from food.

Minerals

The human body depends on 16 different minerals. Zinc helps fight infection. Calcium, magnesium, and phosphorus keep bones strong. Iron helps carry oxygen through the body. Potassium and sodium keep muscles working well, especially the heart. Citrus fruits, nuts, and bananas are high in potassium, while milk and some juices are good sources of calcium.

As with other nutrients, too many or two few minerals can be a problem. For example, too much sodium or salt, combined with too little potassium and calcium, may cause high blood pressure.

Water

Water is essential to a healthy body. The human body needs water to digest food and remove waste. People should aim to drink eight to twelve glasses of water per day.

Taking Responsibility

Each person needs to take responsibility for his or her own health. Eating a variety of nutrient-dense foods is a key step to staying healthy. Sometimes it is hard to know which foods to choose and how much of them to eat.

The food pyramid

The government has created a tool to help people make healthy food choices. The **food pyramid** is made up of six different colored stripes. Each colored stripe stands for a **food group.** The wider the stripe, the more food from its group a person needs to eat each day.

Making food choices can be confusing.

GRAINS | VEGETABLES | FRUITS | MILK | MEAT & BEANS

The girl climbing the food pyramid reminds people to exercise.

Nutrient-dense foods in each food group can be found near the bottom of the food pyramid. Less nutrient-dense foods can be found near the top, along with foods high in sugar and fat. For example, whole grain bread is at the bottom of the grain group. Doughnuts, cookies, and cake are at the top. The shape reminds people to eat more foods from the bottom and fewer from the top.

The food pyramid recommends how much food a person should eat. According to the food pyramid, children aged 9-13 need 3 cups of vegetables, 2 cups of fruit, 3 cups of milk, 5 ounces (140 grams) of meat, and 6 ounces (170 grams) of grains each day. Half of the grains should be whole grains.

Top Tip

The food pyramid measures meat and grains in ounces. How do you know how much makes an ounce? One egg, a quarter-cup of beans, and a tablespoon of peanut butter are each about an ounce. A slice of bread, a half-cup of cooked rice or pasta, a half-cup of cooked cereal, and a cup of cold cereal are also about an ounce.

Nutrition labels

Nutrition fact labels also help people make healthy food choices. These labels are found on packaged food. They show the amount of nutrients in a serving of food.

At the top of each label is a serving size. It is important to check this. Eating more or less than the recommended serving size changes the amount of nutrients a person gets. The serving size also tells a person how much to eat. Next, the label shows how many **calories** are in each serving. Calories are units of energy found in food.

What do you think?

Some schools are banning non-nutrient dense foods such as candy, chips, and cupcakes from parties, concession stands, and fundraisers. They say this will help prevent obesity in young people. Other people say that individuals and families should make their own food decisions. What do you think?

All food labels must give the serving size and show the nutrients the food contains.

Keep Ref

Pasteurized Homogenized

Nutrition Facts

Serving Size 1 cup (236mL)
Servings Per Container 4

Amount Per Serving	Calories from Fat 70
	% Daily Value*
Calories 150	12%
	25%
	10
Total Fat 8g	5
Saturated Fat 5g	
Cholesterol 30mg	
Sodium 120mg	
Total Carbohydrate 11g	
Dietary Fiber 0g	
Sugars 11g	
Protein 8g	

Vitamin
Iron 0%

Vitamin A 4%
Calcium 30%
Vitamin D 25%

* Percent Daily Values are based on a 2,000 calorie d
Your daily values may be higher or lower depending
calorie needs.

		Calories:	2,000	
Total Fat	Less than		65g	
Sat Fat	Less than		20g	
	Less than		300mg	
	Less than		2,400mg	
	Less than		300g	
			25g	

Next comes a list of the nutrients in a serving. These are measured in grams (g), milligrams (mg), and percentages (%). The percentages are based on recommended daily values. The daily value is the amount of the nutrient that an adult should get each day. The label shows the percentage of a nutrient that an adult who eats 2,000 calories a day gets from a serving. For instance, a quarter-cup of tuna fish contains half an ounce (13 grams) of protein. This is 22 percent of an adult's daily protein need. If a serving contains 20 percent or more of a nutrient, it is considered to be high in that nutrient. Five percent or less is considered low.

Food labels also list the amounts of cholesterol, saturated fats, trans fatty acids, and sodium that a food contains. The lower the percentage, the better it is for you.

Comparing food labels can help you choose foods with more nutrients.

Advertising and food choices

Advertising can play a role in food choices. Food advertisements try to make people buy a particular brand of food. They make food look appealing, but rarely tell us its nutritional value.

Advertisers spend $30 billion each year marketing food to children. They often use cartoon characters to advertise high-calorie, non-nutrient dense foods. Some experts say that these ads are one reason that one in seven American children is overweight or **obese.**

Other advertisements feature celebrities. Because people admire celebrities and often want to be like them, they eat the food the celebrities advertise. Food advertisements also show people having fun. These ads make us think that if we eat the advertised food, we will have fun, too.

Some foods, such as french fries, are advertised in a way that makes them attractive to children.

Peer pressure

Peers can also influence what we eat. **Peer pressure** is pressure put on a person by others to behave in a certain way. Peer pressure causes people to do things they might not otherwise do. They do these things to be liked or fit into a group. For example, if a group of young people eats candy and chips at lunch, other young people may do the same thing just to fit in.

Being responsible

Being responsible means making responsible choices. Peer pressure can be very powerful. So can advertisements. That is why it is important to think before eating a food. Does it give you the nutrients you need? Do you really want to eat it, or do your friends or advertisements influence your choice?

Do your friends ever influence your food choices?

Case Study

Not getting enough minerals causes problems. Rob was always tired. A blood test showed that Rob did not have enough red blood cells. These cells carry oxygen to the rest of the body. Rob needed to eat more iron. He added more iron-rich foods such as red meat, whole grains, and eggs to his diet. Soon he was feeling better and had more energy.

How Much Food Is Enough?

Eating larger or smaller **portions** than necessary can affect a person's body. Proper portion size varies from person to person. Active people need more energy to fuel their bodies than inactive people do. A person's age, height, and weight also affect the amount of food and calories he or she needs.

No matter how much people eat, they still may not get all the nutrients they need. Eating a lot of non-nutrient dense foods, such as candy, piles on calories. But non-nutrient dense foods do not supply many nutrients. People need to eat a balance of nutrients to be healthy. This means that people need to get most of their calories from a variety of nutrient-dense foods.

Many foods add on calories without providing a variety of nutrients.

Being active burns calories and helps prevent obesity. Playing volleyball for an hour burns about 286 calories.

Overeating

When people eat more calories than their bodies can use, the extra calories are changed to fat. The fat is stored in their bodies. As more fat is stored, people gain weight. Extra fat can make a person become overweight or obese. These conditions increase a person's chances of heart disease, diabetes, cancer, arthritis, and high blood pressure. In fact, 90 percent of people with type 2 diabetes, an incurable disease, are overweight or obese. So are about one-third of people with high blood pressure.

Top Tip

A 100-pound (45-kilogram) person burns 48 calories per hour, even if he or she is just sitting still. Being active burns even more.

Walking moderately	159 calories
Dancing	272 calories
Skating	318 calories
Bicycling moderately	363 calories
Running five miles per hour	363 calories
Jumping rope	454 calories
Playing soccer	454 calories
Swimming laps	454 calories

Undereating

When people undereat, they take in fewer calories than their bodies need. This causes their bodies to burn muscle tissue and stored fat for energy, which leads to weakness and poor health.

Over time, undereating can cause **malnutrition,** a condition in which the body does not get enough nutrients. A lack of certain vitamins is one symptom of malnutrition. This can cause serious health problems. Severe malnutrition can cause death.

Why do people overeat and undereat?

Many people have no choice about undereating. They cannot afford enough food to keep them healthy. People who do not have problems getting food often undereat to lose weight. They should only do this with the help of a doctor or a registered **dietitian.** That way they can be sure they are still getting all the nutrients they need.

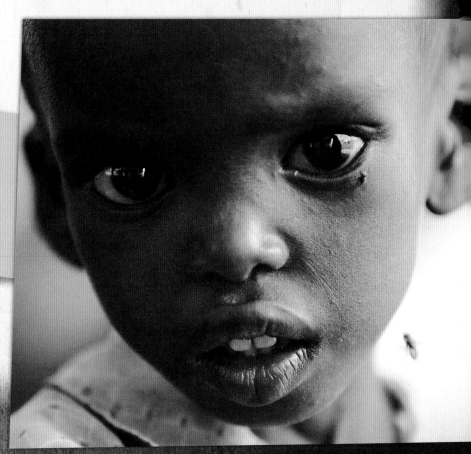

Food shortages lead to malnutrition, and can cause people to starve to death.

When people feel lonely or bored, doing a hobby can keep their minds off eating.

Some people undereat for emotional reasons. **Depression** or **stress** causes them to lose their appetite. To be healthy, these people must eat even when they are feeling upset. Depression and stress can cause other people to overeat. So can loneliness and boredom. Food gives some people comfort. It fills an emptiness they feel. People who are emotional eaters should see their doctor or a registered dietitian for advice.

Dealing with emotional issues helps people change their eating behaviors. Substituting pleasant activities—such as a hobby or a physical activity—for overeating may help too. Seeing a doctor or a registered dietician also helps people maintain proper eating habits.

Top Tip

Not getting enough vitamins can cause problems. For example, a vitamin A deficiency causes vision problems. Deficiencies of some B vitamins can cause weak muscles and skin problems. A vitamin C deficiency causes a disease called scurvy. It also makes it hard to fight infection. A vitamin D deficiency causes weak bones and rickets, a bone disease.

Self-esteem and eating disorders

Low **self-esteem** can cause people to overeat or undereat. Low self-esteem can make people feel they are unattractive. They may become so focused on losing weight that they develop an eating disorder such as **anorexia** or **bulimia.** People with anorexia refuse to eat enough to stay healthy. Those with bulimia eat normally, but take unusual steps to eliminate food from their bodies. They may make themselves vomit, or take laxatives, or exercise too much.

Overeating is an eating disorder that can lead to obesity. In this case, low self-esteem and emotions cause people to overeat. Eating disorders can cause death if not treated. Seeing a doctor can help.

Loneliness or other emotional problems can lead to eating disorders.

Case Study

Jessica was obese. Because she was lonely, she overate. She attended a summer camp for children with eating disorders. She learned healthier ways to deal with her feelings. Special camps are just one of the many ways people with eating disorders can get help.

How much?

One way to know how much to eat is to count calories. Different people have different calorie needs. Depending on his or her height and weight, an active 9- to 13-year-old needs between 1,600 and 2,200 calories each day.

When people count their calorie intake, it is important for them to consider the balance of nutrients as well. The number of calories in a food is not the same as the number of nutrients. For example, both a banana and 1 ounce (28 grams) of jelly beans each have about 105 calories. The banana contains protein, complex carbohydrates, fiber, vitamins, and minerals. The jelly beans contain only simple carbohydrates. Calorie for calorie, the banana gives the body more of what it needs. Most nutrient-dense foods do the same.

Logging on to www.pyramid.gov can help you figure out how many calories you need and help you make nutrient-dense food choices.

Both of these have about the same number of calories, but the nuts also contain protein, fiber, vitamins, and minerals.

Putting it All Together

Eating right can be confusing. It is like putting together a large jigsaw puzzle. It is not easy, but when all the pieces fit, you get a picture of a healthy person.

All foods can fit into a healthy diet. Eating the right amounts of each type of nutrient is the key. Eating mainly non-nutrient dense foods is unhealthy, as is eating foods from just one food group. People need to eat a wide variety of foods to get all the nutrients they need. Non-nutrient dense foods should not be a person's main source of calories, but eating a small amount is fine.

Ice cream is high in fat and calories, but it makes a great treat on special occasions.

NEWSFLASH

The size of containers, plates, and utensils affects how much people eat. As a portion size increases, so does the amount of food people eat. In a study from 2006, scientists found that doubling the size of the bowls increased the amount of ice cream people ate by 31 percent.

Eating five servings of colorful fruits and vegetables every day promotes good health.

Following the portion sizes recommended in the food guide pyramid helps keep people healthy. For example, many fast food and other restaurants offer super-sized portions. But a small order of fries will help satisfy a hunger for fries and still leaves room for more nutrient-dense foods. Sharing a sweet dessert after a nutrient-dense meal is also a good way to enjoy a favorite food and eat in balance.

Top Tip

When we eat, color counts. Brightly colored vegetables and fruits contain phytonutrients, plant substances that improve health. Fruits and vegetables that are blue, purple, and red improve memory. Those that are green build strong bones and teeth and promote good vision. Yellow and orange fight infection and help prevent heart disease. All fruits and vegetables help prevent cancer.

Healthy choices

Everyone's day should start with breakfast. People burn calories even when they sleep. When people get up in the morning, their bodies have gone without food for many hours. They need food to refuel their bodies. Without breakfast, people feel tired. Eating breakfast energizes a person's body. Breakfast also keeps people from overeating during the rest of the day.

Eating a doughnut that contains simple carbohydrates for breakfast will get you going, but not for long. A bowl of oatmeal topped with milk, nuts, and fruit contains complex carbohydrates, protein, vitamins, and minerals. It provides lasting energy.

You do not have to eat a traditional breakfast to get a good start. Any variety of nutrient-rich foods can be eaten for breakfast. A glass of milk and a peanut butter and banana sandwich is a great way to start the day. So is yogurt with fruit and nuts.

NEWSFLASH

Eating breakfast helps students be more alert. Studies have shown that students who eat breakfast do better on math tests than those who do not eat breakfast. They can work longer, have fewer behavioral problems, and are absent and tardy less often than students who skip breakfast.

Students who skip breakfast find it harder to concentrate.

Lunch

Many people eat lunch at school or work. Sack lunches can be delicious and nutrient-dense. A turkey sandwich topped with lettuce on a whole grain roll with milk and a cupful of fresh fruit is a tasty, nutrient-dense lunch. A thermos full of bean soup or meat stew accompanied by a stick of low-fat mozzarella cheese, a piece of cornbread, and an apple is another nutrient-dense choice.

There are many ways to get a variety of nutrients. School cafeterias offer many choices, but not all are nutrient-dense foods. Eating non-nutrient dense foods for lunch piles on calories without providing the nutrients people need.

This delicious lunch is loaded with nutrients.

Dinner

Dinner is a good time for families to gather and share a variety of foods. Pasta topped with tomato sauce and grilled chicken, a green vegetable, and a glass of milk is a tasty, balanced dinner. A juicy pear or other fruit is a healthy dessert. Vegetarians might enjoy a black bean burger on a whole grain bun. Topping it with lettuce and tomato adds vitamins and minerals. A baked potato and a whole-grain roll are nutrient-dense side dishes. For dessert, why not try a scoop of fat-free frozen yogurt topped with berries?

Snacks

Healthy snacking keeps a person's body fueled. However, regular snacking on non-nutrient dense foods such as candy causes low energy. Simple carbohydrates cause blood sugar levels to rise sharply and then drop. This makes people feel tired, and they will need to eat again to raise their energy level.

At home or in restaurants, portion size counts.

Food	Recommended serving	How big is it?
Chicken	1 breast (2-3 oz.)	about the size of a deck of cards
Apple	about 1 cup	about the size of a light bulb
Cheese	2 oz.	about the size of a domino
Pasta	1 cup	about the size of a tennis ball

A tasty snack of air-popped popcorn provides fiber and long-lasting energy.

Snacks such as a hard-boiled egg, turkey or meat cubes, yogurt, and nuts provide protein and long-lasting fuel. Fresh fruits and vegetables provide energy, vitamins, minerals, and fiber. Dipping them in peanut butter, cottage cheese, or hummus adds protein.

Drinks

Water is the healthiest beverage choice. Drinking plenty of water keeps a body working. Nutrient-dense beverages such as real fruit juices are also delicious snacks. Milk and milkshakes made with real fruit and low fat milk provide energy and help strengthen bones. Keeping nutrients in mind helps keep us healthy and tastes delicious.

Top Tips

Make healthy choices when eating at a restaurant by thinking about portion size and how the food you order is prepared. Portion sizes at restaurants are often much larger than what most people need. In addition, freshly prepared foods such as salads or mixed fruit are a healthy choice.

Nutrient Chart

Nutrient	Where can I find it?	What does it do?
Protein	Fish, chicken, beef, pork, eggs, milk, cheese, yogurt, rice, dried beans, peas, lentils, nuts, seeds, wheat, oats, and corn all contain protein.	Most all the parts of our bodies are made from protein. It helps cells to grow and repairs or replaces healthy cells and tissues.
Carbohydrates	Cereals, bread, rice, pasta, potatoes, corn, berries, oranges, and apples all contain carbohydrates. So do many other foods.	Carbohydrates are the body's main source of energy.
Fats	Fat is found in many foods, such as meat and dairy products. We often add fats such as butter, oil, or margarine to foods. Snacks, pastries, and prepared foods often contain fat.	Fat is an important source of calories. Fat also helps carry and store some types of vitamins, such as vitamins A and D.
Vitamins	There are many different types of vitamins, and they are found in different foods. Meat, milk, eggs, fish, whole grains, beans, nuts, green vegetables, and fruit are all good sources of vitamins.	Vitamins have different jobs. Some of them help your body use the energy you get from food. Others help the body build new cells. We need to get enough of some vitamins in order to prevent disease.
Minerals	Different minerals are found in different foods. Meats, whole grains, milk, green vegetables, fruit, beans, cereal, potatoes, seafood, and cheese all contain minerals.	Minerals have different jobs. Calcium helps keep teeth and bones strong, while iron helps form blood cells. Other minerals play a part in healing wounds, helping our nerves, and much more.

How Many Calories?

Making healthy food choices can be confusing. This chart shows some common foods and the number of calories they contain. But remember, calories are only part of the picture. Read food labels carefully and see which nutrients each food contains.

Type of Food	Portion Size	Calories
Apple	1 medium	125
Bagel (plain)	1	200
Banana	1 medium	105
Bologna	2 slices	180
Broccoli, cooked	1 cup (156g)	55
Carrot	1 medium	30
Cheddar cheese	1 oz. (28g)	115
Chicken noodle soup	1 cup (237 ml)	75
Chicken breast, roasted	3 oz. (85g)	140
Chocolate chip cookies	4 cookies	180
Cola, regular	12 fl. oz. (355 ml)	160
Corn flakes	1 oz. (28g)	110
Egg, hard-boiled	1 egg	75
Hamburger	1	245
Ice cream (chocolate)	1 cup (132g)	285
Milk, lowfat (1%)	1 cup (237 ml)	100
Oatmeal	1 cup (80g)	145
Orange juice	1 cup (237 ml)	110
Peanut butter	1 tbsp. (11g)	95
Pizza, plain cheese	1 slice	290
Popcorn, air-popped	1 cup (8g)	30
Potato chips	10 chips	105
Potato, baked	1 medium	220
Tomato soup	1 cup (237 ml)	85
Tuna	3 oz. (85g)	135
Whole wheat bread	1 slice	70

Glossary

amino acid substance that makes up proteins

anorexia eating disorder in which people starve themselves

blood vessel tube in the body that carries blood to tissues and organs

bulimia eating disorder in which people eliminate food by using laxatives, vomiting, or exercising too much

calorie measure of the amount of energy in food

carbohydrate essential nutrient that gives the body energy

cell basic unit of life

depression ongoing feeling of sadness

diabetes incurable disease in which blood sugar levels are higher than normal

dietitian person who is an expert in diet and nutrition

fat essential nutrient that gives the body heat and energy

fiber part of fruits, vegetables, grains, nuts, seeds, and beans that the body cannot digest

food group way to classify foods

food pyramid tool that shows recommended daily food choices

grain seed and fruit of plants such as wheat, corn, rice, barley, and rye

malnutrition condition in which the body does not get enough essential nutrients

mineral essential nutrient such as calcium, iron, magnesium, and potassium

non-nutrient dense containing few nutrients

nutrient substance in food that helps the body to grow and function

nutrient-dense containing many nutrients

obese being more than 20 percent above normal body weight

peer pressure social pressure to behave or look a certain way in order to be accepted by a group

portion serving size

processed food food that contains chemicals and preservatives

protein essential nutrient that is needed for cell repair

saturated fat fat that is solid at room temperature

self-esteem respect for self

stress emotional pressure

trans fatty acid human-made fat found in processed food

unsaturated fat fat that is liquid at room temperature

vegetarian person who does not eat meat products

vitamin essential nutrient that the body needs to be healthy

whole grain grain that has not had any part removed

Further Resources

Books

Ballard, Carol. *Food for Feeling Healthy*. Chicago: Heinemann-Raintree, 2007.

Gray, Shirley Wimbish. *Eating for Good Health*. Mankato, Minn.: The Child's World, 2004.

Koellhoffer, Tara. *Food and Nutrition*. New York: Chelsea Clubhouse, 2006.

Royston, Angela. *Eating*. Chicago: Heinemann-Raintree, 2004.

Websites

CDC "BAM!" (Body and Mind)
www.bam.gov/sub_foodnutrition/index.html

KidsHealth
www.kidshealth.org/kid/

USDA "Eat Smart Play Hard"
www.fns.usda.gov/eatsmartplayhardkids/

MyPyramid.gov
www.pyramid.gov/kids

Organizations

Center for Nutritional Policy and Promotion
3101 Park Center Drive, 10th Floor
Alexandria, VA 22302-1594
(703) 305-7600
Website: www.cnpp.usda.gov

Shape Up America!
6707 Democracy Blvd. Suite 306
Bethesda, MD 20817
Website: www.shapeup.org

Index